HOW TO WRITE A
GREAT SCHOOL REPORT

HOW TO WRITE A GREAT SCHOOL REPORT

ELIZABETH JAMES AND CAROL BARKIN

With an introduction by M. Jean Greenlaw, Ph.D.

LOTHROP, LEE & SHEPARD BOOKS ▪ NEW YORK

PERMISSIONS

The authors are grateful to the following for permission to include copyrighted material in this book:

Pages 20-22 from *The World Book Encyclopedia,* copyright © 1983 by World Book, Inc. Pages 23-25 from *The Hammond Medallion World Atlas,* copyright © 1983 by Hammond, Incorporated, Maplewood, N.J. Pages 28-31 from *The World Almanac & Book of Facts,* 1983 edition, copyright © 1982 by Newspaper Enterprise Association, New York, New York 10166. Page 33 courtesy of The Baker & Taylor Co. Pages 35-36 from *Cats: All About Them* by Alvin and Virginia Silverstein; copyright © 1978 by Alvin Silverstein and Virginia Silverstein; by permission of Lothrop, Lee & Shepard Books (A Division of William Morrow & Company). Page 46 from *Dictionary of Dinosaurs* by Joseph Rosenbloom; copyright © 1980 by Joseph Rosenbloom; by permission of Julian Messner.

And special thanks to Allegra Ressa for her hand-written report.

Designed by Lynn Braswell.

First Edition
6 7 8 9 10

Library of Congress Cataloging in Publication Data

James, Elizabeth.
How to write a great school report.
Includes index.
Summary: Explains how to choose a topic for a report, how to find and organize information, and how to write and revise the final version.
1. Report writing—Juvenile literature. [1. Report writing.   2. Research.   3. English language—Composition and exercises.   4. Homework]   I. Barkin, Carol.   II. Title.
LB1047.3.J34 1983   372.6'23   83–764
ISBN 0–688–02283–9 (lib. bdg.)
ISBN 0–688–02278–2 (pbk.)

Contents

This book is dedicated to all the students who
shared their ideas and experiences with us

TO THE STUDENT

THE TEACHER has just announced that everyone in class is to write a report within the next six weeks. You panic, because you can't think of a single interesting topic. Relax. *How to Write a Great School Report* can help you solve your problem.

James and Barkin begin by describing what a report is and then provide assistance in selecting a topic. They explore the issues of choosing too broad or too narrow a topic and make specific suggestions for deciding upon an idea that will be of interest to you and to your classmates.

Once you have selected a topic, you head straight for the encyclopedia, right? Wrong! Most reports copied from an encyclopedia are quite boring. There are numerous possible sources for your research, and James and Barkin give detailed suggestions for locating these sources and for finding the information you need within them. They also make clear that there are resources beyond books. Museums, television, filmstrips and people in your community are all among the possibilities for research information.

Organization is the secret of a good report. James and Barkin provide you with specific skills for accomplishing this. Deciding what you want and need to know, taking useful notes (not copying), sifting until you have the most important and interesting information, and arranging it into the most appropriate sequence are all clearly discussed. Advice is then given for presenting your report in the most attractive manner that meets the teacher's requirements.

How to Write a Great School Report is filled with clearly written ideas and precise examples. The book is useful, easily read, and quite pleasurable to read.

I highly recommend this book to students, teachers, and parents, all of whom have a concern about producing school reports that are of an excellent quality and that are appealing to the reader.

M. Jean Greenlaw, Ph.D.
Professor of Education
North Texas State University

ONE

What Is a Report?

ALMOST AS SOON as you learn how to write, you start writing reports for school. Writing a report can be a lot of fun. It's your chance to say just what *you* want to say. In third grade you might write about your pet or about an exciting trip you took. In fifth grade you might do a report on a video game you know a lot about or on what it's like to be a newspaper reporter. Putting together a report lets you share what you've learned. And it's much more interesting than filling in the blanks in your workbook!

But what if you don't know how to get started? It can be scary to write something all by yourself. You may feel confused if you don't understand what to do.

A good way to begin is to figure out what a report

really is. Once you get the idea, you'll be able to write a report on any topic.

A report is a collection of information about a topic. It's a way of telling other people what you have found out about the topic. But instead of telling them in spoken words, you're telling them in writing.

Of course, the information in a report must be correct. Suppose you read a report on how to bake a cake. If the directions told you to add one cup of salt and one teaspoon of sugar, that is what you would do. But your cake would taste terrible! You might be pretty mad at the person who wrote down the wrong information. Or suppose you read a social studies report that said there are 48 states in the U.S.A. This used to be true, but it isn't any more. You would know that the writer of this report didn't bother to find the correct information. And you might wonder if the rest of the facts in the report were wrong, too.

But even if all the information is correct, a report is not just a list of facts. Your facts have to be put in order so they make sense. A report on how pioneers made soap is hard to understand if the last steps in soap making are explained before the first steps. Don't confuse your reader! In a report on lizards, the facts about where they live should all be together. The facts about what they eat should go in another section or paragraph. An unorganized jumble of information is no fun to read.

Doing a report is a lot more than writing the sentences and paragraphs. You'll spend as much time gathering your information and organizing it in a logical way as you will writing the actual report. And the better you do each of these steps, the better your report will be in the end.

What makes your report different from someone else's? If teachers assign the same topic to everyone in the class, why don't they get thirty reports that are exactly alike? Because no matter what the topic is, each person thinks about it in his or her own way. Suppose your teacher asks for a report on snow rescue teams. You might wonder what kind of clothes the teams wear on their rescue missions. But your friend wants to know how cold it gets in the mountains. Both of your reports will include some facts about both clothing and weather. But your report won't sound exactly the same as your friend's. The parts of a topic you think are most interesting are the ones you will write the most about. Your view of a topic and your selection of facts makes the report you write your very own—different from everyone else's.

SAMPLE 1.   In early winter it is not very cold in the mountains. The rescue teams wear warm boots and down jackets. They have goggles to keep the sun out of their eyes.

Later it gets really cold. The teams wear ski masks and down hoods. They wear two pairs of mittens. They have thermal socks and special boots. They have to be careful so their fingers and toes don't get frostbite. Sometimes doctors have to cut off frostbitten toes.

SAMPLE 2.   Snow rescue teams work outdoors all winter in the mountains. The rescue teams wear special clothes to keep them warm.

In November and December the daytime temperature is about 25 degrees. At night it drops as low as 0 degrees.

In January and February it gets really cold. It can be lower than 0 degrees during the day. The lowest temperature it ever got was 52 degrees below 0. Even when it's this cold, rescue teams keep on working.

These two reports are on the same topic—snow rescue teams. But the two writers were interested in different details about the teams' work. Each report has a different point of view on the subject. And each gives the reader a new slant or look at the same topic.

This difference is what makes your report yours. When your teacher reads thirty reports on the same subject, none of them will be exactly alike.

TWO

Choosing a Topic

How Do You Decide what to write a report on? First, it should be something you are interested in. You'll do a better job and have more fun if you pick a topic you'd like to learn more about.

But what if your teacher tells the whole class to write about the same thing? This often happens in social studies or science class. You can still make some choices of your own. Almost any topic is too big for a short report. Each person can write about one part of the topic. If the report topic is dinosaurs, there is lots of dinosaur lore that might be fun to explore. Maybe you'd like to know more about where dinosaur bones have been found. Or you might want to find out why dinosaurs became extinct. Types of dinosaurs and what they looked like could be a report topic. Or perhaps you'd like to discuss the information scientists have recently uncovered about the size of Brontosaurus's head.

You can't possibly cover the whole topic of dinosaurs. There is just too much information to be crammed into a school report. Try to choose a topic that is small enough to explain in a few pages.

The whole idea of writing a report is to give some detailed information about a topic. Details make your report interesting to read. Suppose the topic is earthquakes. You might decide to write about major earthquakes all over the world. But you would soon discover that there have been far too many to write about in one report. In fact, there have been more than thirty major earthquakes in this century in the United States alone. Even if you narrowed your topic to include only U.S. earthquakes, you wouldn't have room to do much more than make a list of them. A list like this, even if you wrote it in sentences, would not make a very good report.

But how about writing on the three biggest U.S. earthquakes since 1900? Then you could tell more than just the dates and places where they happened. In your report you could compare the force of the three earthquakes and the amount of damage they caused. Or you might want to report on only one of

NARROWING YOUR TOPIC

EARTHQUAKES

MAJOR EARTHQUAKES AROUND
THE WORLD

MAJOR EARTHQUAKES
IN THE U.S.

THREE MAJOR U.S.
EARTHQUAKES
SINCE
1900

the three biggest earthquakes. If you write about just the Los Angeles earthquake of 1971, you will be able to add many more details to your report. You can tell how many aftershocks there were and how long it took to repair the damage. You might even have room to tell a little about how people's daily lives were changed by the earthquake.

Writing about a smaller portion of a large topic means that you can use more interesting details. This makes a better report. But do be careful not to make your topic *too* small. Then you might not be able to find any information about it. For example, your teacher might tell everyone to write a report on Korea. You must choose which part or aspect of this topic you'd like to write about. Suppose you decide to do your report on the games Korean children play. But when you look for information, you can't find any books that tell about these games.

If you run into this problem, you can make your topic bigger, until you've got something you *can* find out about. For instance, the report on games children play in Korea can be broadened to include other parts of a Korean child's life. You will probably be able to find some information about schools and families, even if you can't find out about games. Once you think of a topic for your report, it is a good idea to talk to your teacher about it. He or she may know how much information is available for you to use.

Whatever topic you choose, make sure it isn't boring to you. Writing a report takes time and lots of work. You won't do your best job if you start out with a topic you don't like.

□ THREE □
Finding Facts

NOW THAT YOU HAVE CHOSEN your topic, you need to gather the information you will put in your report. Digging out the facts is called doing research. It's an important step. If you don't do any research, you won't have anything to write in your report.

Start as early as you can! It may take a while to find the books or magazines you need to look at. And when you've found them, you'll need time to read all those fascinating facts. Besides, when you've finished doing your research, you'll still have the report to write.

Where can you look for information about your topic? Maybe your teacher has brought some books to the classroom for everyone to use. You may be able to find all the information you need in these books. If not, your first stop will be the school or public library.

Before you try to find books on your topic, look it up in some general information books. These are called reference books and are found in the reference section of the library. A reference book is often a good starting point for research.

You may have used an encyclopedia already. It's a set of books that has articles on most subjects that people want to know about. The articles are in alphabetical order. They tell the basic facts about each subject. Encyclopedia articles give some details, but of course they don't have as much information as a whole book on the topic. The last volume is the index to all the other volumes. Look in the index to find which volumes contain articles on your topic. An article on a big topic may be quite long. Look at the headings to find the paragraphs that cover what you want to know. At the end of some articles you may find titles of other articles that tell more about your topic.

It is always a good idea to look in the front of any reference book you are using to find out when it was published. Notice, for instance, that the 1983 *World Book Encyclopedia* article on earthquakes lists major quakes up to 1980. If you need to include a

EARTH SCIENCE is the study of the earth and its origin and development. It deals with the makeup and structure of the earth and with its atmosphere and waters. Earth science is an extremely broad field that combines many related specialties, including geology, meteorology, oceanography, and physical geography.

Earth scientists study the forces that have formed and altered the earth's surface features, both on land and on the ocean floor. For example, movements of the atmosphere and ocean currents affect weather and climate and help shape the earth's surface. Earthquakes, heat production, and other processes within the earth also play a major part in shaping its features. Continued research into such internal forces may lead to the development of techniques to accurately predict earthquakes and volcanic eruptions.

Earth scientists also investigate the distribution of chemical elements in the earth and the processes that produced this distribution. Their findings are often used to locate deposits of metals and minerals important to industry. Other research in earth science involves the study of animal and plant fossils. By analyzing animal and plant fossils, scientists have learned much about the forms of life that existed during different periods in the earth's history. Data from this type of study also provide information about the age of the earth. In addition, such data can be useful in locating deposits of coal, petroleum, and other valuable fossil fuels.   MARIA LUISA CRAWFORD

Related Articles in WORLD BOOK include:

Earth	Geophysics	Ocean
Geochemistry	Hydrology	Paleontology
Geology	Meteorology	Tectonics

EARTHENWARE. See POTTERY.

EARTHQUAKE is a shaking, rolling, or sudden shock of the earth's surface. There may be as many as a million earthquakes in a single year. Most of them take place beneath the surface of the sea. Few of these cause any damage. But earthquakes that occur near large cities cause much damage and loss of life, especially if the cities rest on soft ground. The energy released by a large earthquake may equal that of about 200 million short tons (180 million metric tons) of TNT. In other words, its energy may be 10,000 times as great as that of the first atomic bomb. The strength of an earthquake

Steve McCutcheon

Earthquake Damage results when the moving ground makes buildings shake. Changes in the level of the ground following an earthquake also destroy roads and other structures.

is measured on a scale of numbers called the *Richter Scale* (see RICHTER MAGNITUDE).

Large earthquakes cause violent motions of the earth's surface. Sometimes they cause huge sea waves that sweep up on land and add to the general destruction. Such waves often occur in the Pacific Ocean because of many earthquakes there. Geologists use a Japanese word, *tsunami*, for these destructive waves.

Why Earthquakes Occur. According to the *plate tectonics* theory, the surface of the earth consists of about 20 rigid plates that move slowly past one another. The motion of these plates squeezes and stretches rocks at the edges of the plates. If the force becomes too great, the rocks *rupture* (break) and shift, causing an earthquake. These ruptures are called *faults*. Most faults lie beneath the surface, but some are visible. For example, the San Andreas Fault can be seen in California.

Much of the energy released in an earthquake travels away from the fault in waves called *seismic waves*. Near the *focus* (place where the rupture begins), vibrations

---
MAJOR EARTHQUAKES

Year	Location	Dead	Year	Location	Dead
856	Corinth, Greece	45,000	1920	Kansu Province, China	200,000
1268	Silicia, Asia Minor	60,000	1923	Tokyo-Yokohama, Japan	142,802
1290	Hopeh Province, China	100,000	1932	Kansu Province, China	70,000
1293	Kamakura, Japan	30,000	1935	Quetta, India (now Pakistan)	60,000
1531	Lisbon, Portugal	30,000	1939	Chillan, Chile	30,000
1556	Shensi Province, China	830,000	1960	Agadir, Morocco	12,000
1667	Shemaka, Russia	80,000	1962	Iran	10,000
1693	Catania, Italy	60,000	1964	Alaska	131
1737	Calcutta, India	300,000	1968	Iran	11,588
1755	Northern Persia (now Iran)	40,000	1970	Peru	66,794
1755	Lisbon, Portugal	60,000	1972	Iran	5,374
1759	Baalbek, Lebanon	30,000	1972	Managua, Nicaragua	5,000
1783	Calabria, Italy	50,000	1974	Pakistan	5,200
1797	Quito, Ecuador	41,000	1976	Guatemala	23,000
1828	Echigo, Japan	30,000	1976	Hopeh Province, China	240,000
1906	San Francisco, Calif.	700	1978	Iran	15,000
1908	Messina, Italy	75,000	1980	El Asnam, Algeria	5,000
1915	Avezzano, Italy	29,970	1980	Italy	3,000

Source: National Oceanic and Atmospheric Administration, U.S. Department of Commerce.

EARTHQUAKE

CAUSES AND EFFECTS OF EARTHQUAKES

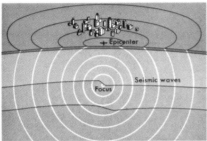

WORLD BOOK diagram by Mas Nakagawa

An Earthquake occurs when forces inside the earth cause a sudden rock movement. The site of the movement is called the *focus* of the quake. Seismic waves created by the quake are strongest at the *epicenter*, the point on the surface above the focus.

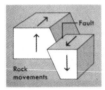
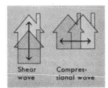

WORLD BOOK diagrams

An Earthquake Focus is centered in rocks that have broken and slid past one another. Geologists call such places *faults*.

Seismic Waves include *shear waves*, which shake buildings vertically, and *compressional waves*, which move them horizontally.

of the seismic waves can be destructive. Seismographic stations throughout the world record seismic waves from a great earthquake (see SEISMOLOGY).

Seismic waves consist of compressional waves, shear waves, and surface waves. *Compressional* (longitudinal) *waves* are really sound waves, and travel at a speed of 5 miles (8 kilometers) a second. The rocks vibrate in the direction traveled by the wave. This causes the rocks to change volume. *Shear* (transverse) *waves* travel about half as fast as compressional waves. The rocks vibrate at right angles to the direction traveled by the wave. This causes the rocks to change shape. *Surface waves* travel slightly slower than shear waves. They are confined to the earth's surface in much the same way that ocean waves are limited to the surface of the sea.

Seismic waves pass directly through the earth in about 21 minutes. By measuring their speed, scientists can obtain some idea of the kinds of rocks that are found below the surface of the earth.

Location of Earthquakes. Seismologists locate earthquakes by studying the time intervals at which the different seismic waves reach a number of seismographic stations (see SEISMOGRAPH). They draw circles on a map to show the distance of the earthquake from each of the stations. The earthquake is located where the circles intersect one another. The focus of most earthquakes occurs less than 25 miles (40 kilometers) beneath the surface of the earth. A few take place at the earth's surface, and some may occur at depths as great as 400 miles (640 kilometers).

Most earthquakes occur along the boundaries where plates separate, collide, or slide past each other. These places are the earth's most geologically active regions. Volcanoes, new mountain ranges, and deep ocean trenches—in addition to earthquakes—occur along the edges of the plates. In contrast, the flat parts of the continents and sea floor are stable regions that have few quakes. Most earthquakes take place within two belts. The *circum-Pacific* belt lies along plate boundaries around the Pacific Ocean. The *Alpide* belt follows plate boundaries across southern Europe and Asia.

Prediction of Earthquakes is not yet possible, but scientists are optimistic that they will find a method. Scientists know the regions where earthquakes are likely to occur. They may use the history of previous earthquakes to guess how often a certain region may expect earthquakes. For example, California may expect a catastrophic earthquake once every 50 to 100 years. In such regions, engineers have developed buildings that can withstand the severest earthquakes.

Some seismologists, in an effort to predict when earthquakes may occur, have experimented with devices that record small movements along a fault. Others

WHERE EARTHQUAKES OCCUR

Almost all the world's major earthquakes occur in two great belts — the circum-Pacific belt and the Alpide belt. Each dot on the map represents five earthquakes during a nine-year period. The circum-Pacific belt, sometimes called the *Ring of Fire*, accounts for more than three-fourths of the world's earthquakes. Most of the other quakes occur in the Alpide belt, which cuts across Europe and Asia from Burma to southern Europe and North Africa. Other active earthquake areas include the mid-oceanic ridges that form undersea mountain chains.

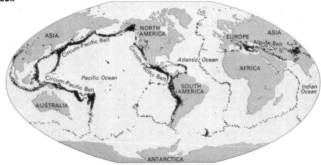

Earthworm   **The Earthworm's Body** is made up of segments. On each segment, except the first and last, are four pairs of tiny bristles called *setae* that help the worm move through the earth.

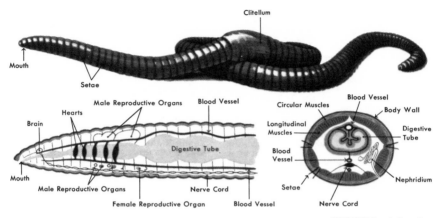

Clitellum

Mouth

Setae

Male Reproductive Organs   Blood Vessel   Circular Muscles   Blood Vessel

Hearts   Body Wall

Brain   Longitudinal Muscles   Digestive Tube

Digestive Tube   Blood Vessel

Mouth   Nephridium

Male Reproductive Organs   Nerve Cord   Setae

Female Reproductive Organ   Blood Vessel   Nerve Cord

WORLD BOOK diagrams by Margaret Estey

An Earthworm Has Five Pairs of "Hearts" in the front part of its body. The "hearts" help circulate the worm's blood.

A Worm's Waste Matter is given off by organs called *nephridia,* which function like human kidneys.

have measured the speed of the seismic waves produced by small quakes or explosive charges. Both methods have been somewhat successful in predicting earthquakes. But more research and experimentation are needed before anyone can predict exactly when and where an earthquake will occur.

Damage by Earthquakes. Most earthquakes pass without being noticed. Light earthquakes may easily be mistaken for the rumbling of a truck. But large, destructive earthquakes do occur from time to time. Most of the destruction takes place shortly after the first tremor of the earthquake is felt.

Most earthquake damage, such as falling rubble, is indirect. The earthquake shakes a building and loosens the bricks in a chimney or wall. They fall, injuring someone. Earthquakes may also damage water pipes, electric lines, and gas mains. Fire is probably the greatest single danger in an earthquake.   FRANK PRESS

Related Articles in WORLD BOOK include:

Continental Drift	San Andreas Fault
Earth	San Francisco (History)
Flood (Seacoast Floods)	Seismograph
Japan (The Land)	Seismology
Mediterranean	Tectonics
Sea (The Seabed)	

Additional Resources

BOLT, BRUCE. *Earthquakes: A Primer.* Freeman, 1978.
DeNEVI, DON. *Earthquakes.* Celestial Arts, 1977.
EIBY, GEORGE A. *Earthquakes.* Van Nostrand, 1980.
HALACY, DANIEL S. *Earthquakes: A Natural History.* Bobbs, 1974.
HODGSON, JOHN H. *Earthquakes and Earth Structure.* Prentice-Hall, 1964.

EARTHSHINE. See MOON (The Phases of the Moon; diagram).

EARTHWORM, also called NIGHT CRAWLER, is a common worm found in moist, warm soil in many parts of the world. The earthworm is a well-known bait used by fishermen, and is sometimes called a *fishworm* or *angleworm.*

Earthworms contribute to the growth of plants. The worms help break down the *humus* (decaying matter in the soil). The air necessary for plant growth enters the soil through burrows the earthworm has dug in the soil. Worms are also important food for birds.

Earthworms range in size from those that are only $\frac{1}{25}$ inch (1 millimeter) long to those that are up to 11 feet (3 meters) long. They have a smooth body that is made up of rings called *annuli.* The reddish-brown body of the earthworm is built like two tubes, one inside the other. The inner one is the digestive tube and the outer one is the body wall. Earthworms do not have eyes or ears, but they have a mouth and are sensitive to heat, light, and touch.

A worm crawls by lengthening its front part and pushing through the soil, then pulling the hind part up. A worm's body wall has two kinds of muscles that it uses to crawl. Circular muscles surround the worm's body and can make the body shrink or spread out. Longitudinal muscles run the length of the body and can shorten or lengthen the worm. *Setae* (bristles) prevent the worm from slipping.

The earthworm has no lungs or gills. It breathes through its thin skin, which is in contact with the air between the particles of soil. When it rains these air spaces fill with water and earthworms then must either come to the surface or drown. If the weather becomes too dry and warm, a worm will die. Earthworms feed on dead plant material that is found in the soil. This is why some people say an earthworm eats its way through the soil.

An earthworm has both male and female reproductive organs, but each worm must mate with another

21

more recent quake in your report, you will have to do further research. Ask your librarian to recommend a reliable source for up-to-date information.

What other reference books can you use? An atlas is a book of maps, but it also has lots of other information. It lists the populations of countries and big cities. It may give facts about climate, time zones, crops, and many other topics. For a report on weather systems around the world or the principal resources of your state, an atlas may have much of the information you need. For any report that deals with physical information about the United States or the world, an atlas is a good place to check for information.

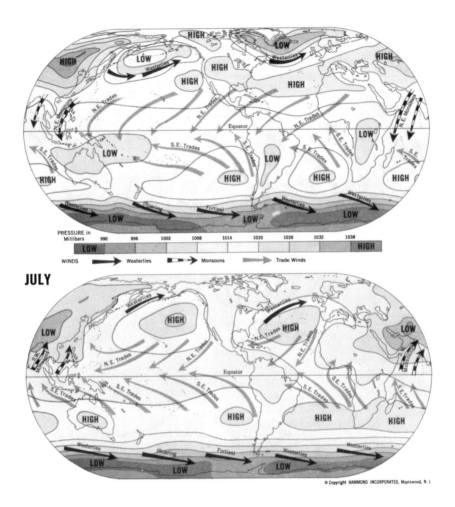

| PRESSURE in Millibars | 990 | 996 | 1002 | 1008 | 1014 | 1020 | 1026 | 1032 | 1038 |

LOW   HIGH

WINDS   ➡ Westerlies   ⟿ Monsoons   ⟹ Trade Winds

JULY

AIR PRESSURE
AND WINDS

Just as the atmosphere tends to equalize heat
distribution, it tends to maintain equal pressure
over the earth. Whenever this equilibrium, or
balance, is disturbed, air flows from areas of
higher pressure to areas of lower pressure. In the
Northern Hemisphere winds flow clockwise around
a high pressure area (high) and counterclockwise
around the center of a low pressure area (low).
These movements are reversed in the Southern
Hemisphere.

MASSACHUSETTS
AREA 8,257 sq. mi.
POPULATION 5,689,170
CAPITAL Boston
LARGEST CITY Boston
HIGHEST POINT Mt. Greylock 3,491 ft.
SETTLED IN 1620
ADMITTED TO UNION February 6, 1788
POPULAR NAME Bay State; Old Colony
STATE FLOWER Mayflower
STATE BIRD Chickadee

RHODE ISLAND
AREA 1,214 sq. mi.
POPULATION 949,723
CAPITAL Providence
LARGEST CITY Providence
HIGHEST POINT Jerimoth Hill 812 ft.
SETTLED IN 1636
ADMITTED TO UNION May 29, 1790
POPULAR NAME Little Rhody
STATE FLOWER Violet
STATE BIRD Rhode Island Red

Agriculture, Industry and Resources

WORCESTER
Machinery, Metal Products, Machine Tools, Wire & Abrasives, Textiles, Leather Goods

FITCHBURG–LEOMINSTER
Paper & Plastic Products, Machinery, Textiles

LOWELL
Textiles, Leather Goods, Electrical Products

LAWRENCE–HAVERHILL
Textiles, Shoes, Metal Products, Rubber Goods

BOSTON
Electrical & Metal Products, Electronic Equipment, Machinery, Food Processing, Printing & Publishing, Leather Goods, Textiles, Shipbuilding

PITTSFIELD
Electrical Machinery, Textiles

BROCKTON
Shoes, Leather, Textiles

SPRINGFIELD–HOLYOKE
Machinery, Metal Products, Ordnance, Chemicals, Paper Products, Textiles

PROVIDENCE
Textiles, Clothing, Jewelry & Silverware, Machinery, Nonferrous Metals, Metal Products

FALL RIVER
Clothing, Textiles, Rubber Products

NEW BEDFORD
Textiles, Clothing, Machinery

DOMINANT LAND USE

- Specialized Dairy
- Dairy, Poultry, Mixed Farming
- Forests
- Urban Areas

MAJOR MINERAL OCCURRENCES

Granite

Water Power   Major Industrial Areas

(continued on following page)

Another helpful reference book is a yearly almanac. Almanacs are fat books that are filled with odd and unusual facts. An almanac may contain a brief history of the United States and of the world, sports statistics, information about pets, descriptions of all the national parks, and lots more. When you have some spare time, you might want to glance through an almanac; you'll be amazed at all the strange things you can find out.

As you do your research, you may come across words you don't understand. A dictionary will tell you what they mean and how to pronounce them. Many of the larger ("unabridged") dictionaries also have color pictures of things like state flags, birds, and precious stones.

After you've seen what the reference books have to say about your topic, you are ready to read more. Encyclopedias give the basic facts. Now you need books that give many more details. How can you find them?

All libraries are set up pretty much the same way. The books are divided into fiction and nonfiction. Fiction books have stories in them; nonfiction books have facts. Fiction is arranged in alphabetical order according to the author's last name. The shelves that hold the fiction books usually have letters on them, such as "A–B," so you know where to start looking for the book you want.

Nonfiction is arranged differently. There are so many nonfiction books on different subjects in a library that they have to be arranged by topic. If they were put in order alphabetically by author, books on one topic would be scattered all over the library. If you wanted to find a book on the solar system, you would have no idea where to look. Putting all the books on one topic together makes it easy to find information about that topic.

Each nonfiction book in the library has a label with a number on it. The number tells what topic the book is about. This method of using numbers to organize nonfiction books was invented by Melvil Dewey; it is the Dewey Decimal Classification System.

All the books with the same number are gathered together on the same library shelf. The shelves of nonfiction books usually have numbers on them, such as "500–599," so you know where to start looking for the books you want. For example, all the 500 books are about science. All the 551.2 books are about the smaller topic of earthquakes. If you wanted to locate a book about earthquakes, you would look for books labeled with the number 551.2.

But how do you know what number your topic

Construction Details of Large and Unusual Bridges

Verrazano-Narrows Bridge, between Staten Island and Brooklyn, N.Y., has a suspension span of 4,260 ft., exceeding the Golden Gate Bridge, San Francisco, by 60 ft. One level in use Nov., 1964, second opened Jun. 28, 1969. The name is a compromise; it spans the Narrows and commemorates a visit to New York Harbor in Apr., 1524, deduced from certain notes left by Giovanni da Verrazano, Italian navigator sailing for Francis I of France.

Allegheny River Bridge (Interstate 80) near Emlenton, Pa., 270 ft. above the water, tallest in eastern U.S., a continuous truss, 688 ft. long, 1968.

Angostura, suspension type, span 2,336 feet, 1967 at Ciudad Bolivar, Venezuela. Total length, 5,507.

Charles Braga Bridge over Taunton River between Fall River and Somerset, Mass. It is 5,780 feet long.

Bendorf Bridge on the Rhine River, 5 mi. n. of Coblenz, completed 1965, is a 3-span cement girder bridge, 3,378 ft. overall length, 101 ft. wide, with the main span 682 ft.

Burro Creek Bridge with 4 spans over Burro Creek on highway 93 near Kingman, Ariz. Main span steel truss 680 ft. Others plate girder, 110 and 2 of 85 ft. 1966.

Champlain Bridge at Montreal crossing the St. Lawrence River was opened 1962. It is 4 miles long.

Chesapeake Bay Bridge-Tunnel, opened Apr. 15, 1964 on US-13, connects Virginia Beach-Norfolk with the Eastern Shore of Virginia. Shore to shore, 17.6 miles. Twelve miles of trestles, 4 man-made islands, 2 mile-long tunnels, and 2 bridges.

Cross Bay Parkway Bridge (N.Y.), 3,000 feet long with 6 traffic lanes, 11 eight foot wide precast, prestressed concrete T girders to support spans 130 feet long each with main span 275 feet.

Delaware Memorial Bridge over Delaware River near Wilmington. A twin suspension bridge paralleling the original 250 ft. upstream has a 2,150-ft. main span suspended from 440-ft. towers.

Eads Bridge across the Mississippi R. between St. Louis and E. St. Louis, built in 1874 has 4 main spans 1,520 ft., 2,502 ft., and 1,118 ft. crossing Miss. R., a railroad and a road.

Evergreen Point Bridge, Wash. consists of 33 floating concrete pontoons weighing 4,700 tons each, held in place by 77 ton crete anchors. Pontoon structure is 6,561 ft. long; with approaches bridge is 12,596 ft. long.

Fremont Bridge. Part of Stadium Freeway, Portland, Ore., crossing Willamette R. 1,255 ft. steel arch span with two 452 ft. flanking steel arch spans. 1971.

Frontenac Bridge, Quebec, suspension, span 2,190 ft., open 1970.

Gladesville Bridge at Sydney, Australia, has the longest concrete arch in the world (1,000-ft. span).

George Washington Bridge, New York City, 4th longest suspension bridge in the world, spans the Hudson River between W. 178th St., Manhattan, and Ft. Lee, N.J.; 4,760 ft. between anchorages, two levels, 14 traffic lanes. Triborough Bridge connects Manhattan, the Bronx, and Queens; project comprises a suspension bridge, a vertical lift bridge, and a fixed bridge, all connected by long viaducts. The famous Brooklyn Bridge over the East River, connecting Manhattan and Brooklyn, was completed in 1883, breaking all previous records by spanning 1,595 ft.

Golden Gate Bridge, crossing San Francisco Bay, has the second longest single span, 4,200 ft.

Hampton Roads Bridge-Tunnel, Va. A crossing completed in 1957 consisting of 2 man-made islands, 2 concrete trestle bridges, and one tunnel, under Hampton Roads with a length of 7,479 ft. A parallel facility with a 7,315 ft. tunnel is now open to traffic.

Hood Canal Floating Bridge, Wash., 23 floating concrete pontoons 4,980 tons each. Roadway is supported on crete T-beam sections mounted on pontoons 20 feet above canal. Floating section is 6,471 ft. long, overall 7,866 ft. Closed Feb. 13, 1979; severe storm damage.

Humber Bridge, with a suspension span of 4,626 ft., the longest in the world, crosses the Humber estuary 5 miles west of the city of Kingston upon Hull, England. Unique in a large suspension bridge are the towers of reinforced concrete instead of steel.

International Bridge, a series of 8 arch and truss bridges crossing St. Mary's and the Soo Locks between Mich. and Ontario. Two-mile toll completed 1962.

Lacy V. Murrow Floating Bridge, Wash., 25 floating pontoons of 4,558 tons each. Bridge with approaches is 8,583 ft.

Lake Pontchartrain Twin Causeway, a twin-span crete trestle bridge and 24-mile link within metropolitan New Orleans that connects the north and south shore. First span opened 1956, second 1969.

Lavaca Bay Causeway, Tex., 2.2 miles long, consisting of one 260 ft. continuous plate girder unit and 194 precast, prestressed concrete spans of 60 ft. length. 1961.

Newport Bridge between Newport and Jamestown, R.I. Total length 11,248 ft., a main suspension span of 1,600 feet, 2 side spans each 688 feet long. It has U.S.A.'s first prefabricated wire strands.

New York City bridges, *see Verrazano-Narrows Bridge and George Washington Bridge above.*

Ogdensburg-Prescott Internat'l Bridge across the St. Lawrence River from Ogdensburg, N.Y., to Johnston, Ont., opened 1970, is 13,510 ft. long with approaches and 7,260 ft. between abutments.

Oland Island Bridge in Sweden was completed in 1972. It is 19,882 feet long, Europe's longest.

Oosterscheldebrug, opened Dec. 15, 1965, is a 3.125-mile causeway for automobiles over a sea arm in Zeeland, the Netherlands. It completes a direct connection between Flushing and Rotterdam.

Poplar St. Bridge over the Mississippi at St. Louis, a 5-span continuous orthotropic deck plate girder bridge, longest span 600 ft. Eight lanes, 2,165 ft. long.

Quebec Road, suspension, span 2,190 feet, 1969, Quebec, Canada.

Rio-Niteroi, Guanabara Bay, Brazil, under construction, will be world's longest continuous box and plate girder bridge, 8 miles, 3,363 feet long, with a center span of 984 feet and a span on each side of 656 feet.

Robert Opie Norris Bridge, Rappahannock R. between Greys Pt. and White Stone, Va. 9,989 ft. long. Main spans are two 144 foot cantilever truss spans with a 360 foot truss span suspended between them.

Rockville Bridge, world's longest 4-track stone arch bridge, 3,810 ft., with 48 arches. Part of the Consolidated Rail Corp. system west of Harrisburg, Pa. It contains 440 million lbs. of stone, 100,000 cubic yds. of masonry and crosses the Susquehanna Riv. to Rockville, Pa.

Royal Gorge Bridge, 1,053 ft. above the Arkansas River in Colorado, is the highest bridge above water. Opened Dec. 8, 1929, it is 1,260 ft. long with a main span of 880 ft., width 18 ft.

San Mateo-Hayward Bridge across San Francisco Bay is first major orthotropic bridge in U.S. It is 6.7 miles long, 4.9 mile low-level concrete trestle and 1.8 miles high-level steel bridge.

Seven Mile Bridge is the longest of an expanse of bridges connecting the Florida Keys. It was built by the Florida East Coast Railway between 1904 and 1916, now a state highway.

Shenandoah River Bridges, one spans the south fork, 1,924 ft. long, the other the north fork, 1,090 ft. long. Warren County, Va.

Straits of Mackinac Bridge, completed in 1957, is the longest suspension bridge between anchorages and with approaches extends nearly 5 mi. between Mackinaw City and St. Ignace, Mich.

Sunshine Skyway, a 15-mile-long bridge-causeway with twin roadbeds that crosses Tampa Bay at St. Petersburg, Fla., a system of twin bridges 864 feet long and 4 smaller bridges with 6 causeways. The main span of the south bound bridge was torn away May 9, 1980, when support tower was hit by a cargo ship.

Tagus River Bridge near Lisbon, Portugal, longest suspension bridge outside the United States, has a 3,323-ft. main span. Opened Aug. 6, 1966, it was named Salazar Bridge for the former premier.

Thomas A. Edison Memorial Bridge (causeway) across Sandusky Bay between Martin Point and Danbury, Oh., is 2.67 miles long. The main bridge is 2,044 feet long.

Thousand Island Bridge, St. Lawrence River. American span 800 ft.; Canadian 750 ft.

Union St. Bridge in Woodstock, Vt., a timber lattice truss with a span of 122 feet built in 1969 using old time procedure of hand drilled holes and wooden pegs.

Vancouver Bridge, Canada's longest railway lift span connecting Vancouver and North Vancouver over Burrard Inlet. It is in 3 sections, the longest 493 ft. Spans are part of a project that includes a 2-mile tunnel under Vancouver Hts.

Woodrow Wilson Memorial Bridge across the Potomac River at Alexandria, Va., is over a mile long.

Zoo Bridge across the Rhine at Cologne, with steel box girders, has a main span of 850 ft.

The Interstate Highway 610 crossing of the Houston Ship Channel in Texas is 6,300 feet in length and consists of various lengths of prestressed concrete beam and slab approach spans and a 1,233 foot main unit of two 471'6" plate girder units and one 290 ft. simple span.

Underwater Vehicular Tunnels in North America

(3,000 feet in length or more)

Name	Location	Waterway	Lgth. Ft.
Bart Trans-Bay Tubes (Rapid Transit)	San Francisco, Cal.	S.F. Bay	3.6 miles
Brooklyn-Battery	New York, N.Y.	East River	9,117
Holland Tunnel	New York, N.Y.	Hudson River	8,557
Lincoln Tunnel	New York, N.Y.	Hudson River	8,216
Baltimore Harbor Tunnel	Baltimore, Md.	Patapsco River	7,650
Hampton Roads	Norfolk, Va.	Hampton Roads	7,479
Queens Midtown	New York, N.Y.	East River	6,414
Thimble Shoal Channel	Cape Henry, Va.	Chesapeake Bay	5,738
Sumner Tunnel	Boston, Mass.	Boston Harbor	5,650
Chesapeake Channel	Cape Charles, Va.	Chesapeake Bay	5,450
Louis-Hippolyte Lafontaine Tunnel	Montreal, Que.	St. Lawrence River	5,280
Detroit-Windsor	Detroit, Mich.	Detroit River	5,135
Callahan Tunnel	Boston, Mass.	Boston Harbor	5,046
Midtown Tunnel	Norfolk, Va.	Elizabeth River	4,194
Baytown Tunnel	Baytown, Tex.	Houston Ship Channel	4,111
Posey Tube	Oakland, Cal.	Oakland Estuary	3,500
Downtown Tunnel	Norfolk, Va.	Elizabeth River	3,350
Webster St.	Alameda, Cal.	Oakland Estuary	3,350
Bankhead Tunnel	Mobile, Ala.	Mobile River	3,109
I-10 Twin Tunnel	Mobile, Ala.	Mobile River	3,000

Land Vehicular Tunnels in U.S.

(over 1,200 feet in length.)

Name	Location	Lgth. Ft.	Name	Location	Lgth. Ft.
Eisenhower Memorial	Route 70, Col.	8,941	F.D. Roosevelt Dr.	81-89 Sts. N.Y.C.	2,400
Copperfield	Copperfield, Ut.	6,989	Dewey Sq.	Boston, Mass.	2,400
Allegheny (twin)	Penna. Turnpike	6,070	Battery Park	N.Y.C.	2,300
Liberty Tubes	Pittsburgh, Pa.	5,920	Battery St.	Seattle, Wash.	2,140
Zion Natl. Park	Rte. 9, Utah	5,766	Big Oak Flat	Yosemite Natl. Park	2,083
East River Mt. (twin)	Interstate 77, W. Va.-Va.	5,661	Carlin	I-80, Nev.	1,993
Tuscarora (twin)	Penna. Turnpike	5,326	Prudential	Boston, Mass.	1,980
Kittatinny (twin)	Penna. Turnpike	4,727	Internatl. Underpass	Los Angeles, Cal.	1,910
Lehigh	Penna. Turnpike	4,379	Street-Car	Providence, R.I.	1,793
Blue Mountain (twin)	Penna. Turnpike	4,339	Broadway	San Francisco, Cal.	1,616
Wawona	Yosemite Natl. Park	4,233	9th Street Expy.	Washington, D.C.	1,610
Squirrel Hill	Pittsburgh, Pa.	4,225	F.D. Roosevelt Dr.	42-48 Sts. N.Y.C.	1,600
Big Walker Mt.	Route I-77, Va.	4,200	Lowry Hill	Minneapolis.	1,496
Fort Pitt	Pittsburgh, Pa.	3,560	Wheeling	Interstate 70, W. Va.	1,490
Mall Tunnel	Dist. of Columbia	3,400	Mt. Baker Ridge (3)	Seattle, Wash.	1,466
Caldecott	Oakland, Cal.	3,371	Knowls Creek	Lane County, Ore.	1,430
Cody No. 1	U.S. 14, 16, 20, Wyo.	3,224	Mule Pass	Near Bisbee, Ariz.	1,400
Kalihi	Honolulu, Ha.	2,780	Arch Cape	Oregon Coast Hwy. 9	1,228
Memorial	W. Va. Tpke. (I-77)	2,669	Queen Creek	Superior, Ariz.	1,200
Cross-Town	178 St. N.Y.C.	2,414	West Rock	New Haven, Conn.	1,200

World's Longest Railway Tunnels

Source: Railway Directory & Year Book 1980. Tunnels over 4.9 miles in length.

Tunnel	Date	Miles	Yds	Operating railway	Country
Dai-shimizu	1979	13	1,384	Japanese National	Japan
Simplon No. 1 and 2	1906, 1922	12	546	Swiss Fed. & Italian St.	Switz.-Italy
Kanmon	1975	11	1,093	Japanese National	Japan
Apennine	1934	11	881	Italian State	Italy
Rokko	1972	10	158	Japanese National	Japan
Gotthard	1882	9	552	Swiss Federal	Switzerland
Lotschberg	1913	9	130	Bern-Lotschberg-Simplon	Switzerland
Hokuriku	1962	8	1,079	Japanese National	Japan
Mont Cenis (Frejus)	1871	8	847	Italian State	France-Italy
Shin-Shimizu	1961	8	675	Japanese National	Japan
Aki	1975	8	161	Japanese National	Japan
Cascade	1929	7	1,388	Burlington Northern	U.S.
Flathead	1970	7	1,319	Great Northern	U.S.
Keijo	1970	7	88	Japanese National	Japan
Lierasen	1973	6	1,135	Norwegian State	Norway
Santa Lucia	1977	6	656	Italian State	Italy
Arlberg	1884	6	643	Austrian Federal	Austria
Moffat	1928	6	366	Denver & Rio Grande Western	U.S.
Shimizu	1931	6	44	Japanese National	Japan
Kvineshei	1943	5	1,107	Norwegian State	Norway
Bigo	1975	5	927	Japanese National	Japan
Rimutaka	1955	5	816	New Zealand Gov.	New Zealand
Ricken	1910	5	603	Swiss Federal	Switzerland
Kaimai	1978	5	873	New Zealand Gov.	New Zealand
Grenchenberg	1915	5	575	Swiss Federal	Switzerland
Otira	1923	5	559	New Zealand Gov.	New Zealand
Tauern	1909	5	546	Austrian Federal	Austria
Haegebostad	1943	5	462	Norwegian State	Norway
Ronco	1889	5	272	Italian State	Italy
Hauenstein (Lower)	1916	5	90	Swiss Federal	Switzerland
Connaught	1916	5	34	Canadian Pacific	Canada
Karawanken	1906	4	1,677	Austrian Federal	Austria-Yugo.
Kobe	1972	4	1,671	Japanese National	Japan
New Tanna	1964	4	1,658	Japanese National	Japan

Major Earthquakes

Magnitude of earthquakes (Mag.), distinct from deaths or damage caused, is measured on the Richter scale, on which each higher number represents a tenfold increase in energy measured in ground motion. Adopted in 1935, the scale has been applied in the following table to earthquakes as far back as reliable seismograms are available.

Date	Place	Deaths	Mag.
526 May 20	Syria, Antioch	250,000	N.A.
856	Greece, Corinth	45,000	"
1057	China, Chihli	25,000	"
1268	Asia Minor, Cilicia	60,000	"
1290 Sept. 27	China, Chihli	100,000	"
1293 May 20	Japan, Kamakura	30,000	"
1531 Jan. 26	Portugal, Lisbon	30,000	"
1556 Jan. 24	China, Shaanxi	830,000	"
1667 Nov.	Caucasia, Shemaka	80,000	"
1693 Jan. 11	Italy, Catania	60,000	"
1730 Dec. 30	Japan, Hokkaido	137,000	"
1737 Oct. 11	India, Calcutta	300,000	"
1755 June 7	Northern Persia	40,000	"
1755 Nov. 1	Portugal, Lisbon	60,000	8.75*
1783 Feb. 4	Italy, Calabria	30,000	N.A.
1797 Feb. 4	Ecuador, Quito	41,000	N.A.
1822 Sept. 5	Asia Minor, Aleppo	22,000	N.A.
1828 Dec. 28	Japan, Echigo	30,000	"
1868 Aug. 13-15	Peru and Ecuador	40,000	"
1875 May 16	Venezuela, Colombia	16,000	"
1896 June 15	Japan, sea wave	27,120	"
1906 Apr. 18-19	Cal., San Francisco	452	8.3
1906 Aug. 16	Chile, Valparaiso	20,000	8.6
1908 Dec. 28	Italy, Messina	83,000	7.5
1915 Jan. 13	Italy, Avezzano	29,980	7.5
1920 Dec. 16	China, Gansu	100,000	8.6
1923 Sept. 1	Japan, Tokyo	99,330	8.3
1927 May 22	China, Nan-Shan	200,000	8.3
1932 Dec. 26	China, Gansu	70,000	7.6
1933 Mar. 2	Japan	2,990	8.9
1934 Jan. 15	India, Bihar-Nepal	10,700	8.4
1935 May 31	India, Quetta	30,000	7.5
1939 Jan. 24	Chile, Chillan	28,000	8.3
1939 Dec. 26	Turkey, Erzincan	30,000	7.9
1946 Dec. 21	Japan, Honshu	2,000	8.4
1948 June 28	Japan, Fukui	5,131	7.3
1949 Aug. 5	Ecuador, Pelileo	6,000	6.8
1950 Aug. 15	India, Assam	1,530	8.7
1953 Mar. 18	NW Turkey	1,200	7.2
1956 June 10-17	N. Afghanistan	2,000	7.7
1957 July 2	Northern Iran	2,500	7.4
*1957 Dec. 13	Western Iran	2,000	7.1
1960 Feb. 29	Morocco, Agadir	12,000	5.8
1960 May 21-30	Southern Chile	5,000	8.3
1962 Sept. 1	Northwestern Iran	12,230	7.1
1963 July 26	Yugoslavia, Skopje	1,100	6.0
1964 Mar. 27	Alaska	114	8.5
1966 Aug. 19	Eastern Turkey	2,520	6.9
1968 Aug. 31	Northeastern Iran	12,000	7.4
1970 Mar. 28	Western Turkey	1,086	7.4
1970 May 31	Northern Peru	66,794	7.7
1971 Feb. 9	Cal., San Fernando Valley	65	6.5
1972 Apr. 10	Southern Iran	5,057	6.9
1972 Dec. 23	Nicaragua	5,000	6.2
1974 Dec. 28	Pakistan (9 towns)	5,200	6.3
1975 Sept. 6	Turkey (Lice, etc.)	2,312	6.8
1976 Feb. 4	Guatemala	22,778	7.5
1976 May 6	Northeast Italy	946	6.5
1976 June 26	New Guinea, Irian Jaya	443	7.1
1976 July 28	China, Tangshan	800,000	8.2
1976 Aug. 17	Philippines, Mindanao	8,000	7.8
1976 Nov. 24	Eastern Turkey	4,000	7.9
1977 Mar. 4	Romania, Bucharest, etc.	1,541	7.5
1977 Aug. 19	Indonesia	200	8.0
1977 Nov. 23	Northwestern Argentina	100	8.2
1978 June 12	Japan, Sendai	21	7.5
1978 Sept. 16	Northeast Iran	25,000	7.7
1979 Sept. 12	Indonesia	100	8.1
1979 Dec. 12	Colombia, Ecuador	800	7.9
1980 Oct. 10	Northwestern Algeria	4,500	7.3
1980 Nov. 23	Southern Italy	4,800	7.2

(*) estimated from earthquake intensity. (N.A.) not available.

Floods, Tidal Waves

Date	Location	Deaths
1887	Huang He River, China	900,000
1889 May 31	Johnstown, Pa.	2,200
1900 Sept. 8	Galveston, Tex.	5,000
1903 June 15	Heppner, Ore.	325
1911	Chang Jiang River, China	100,000
1913 Mar. 25-27	Ohio, Indiana	732
1915 Aug. 17	Galveston, Tex.	275
1928 Mar. 13	Collapse of St. Francis Dam, Santa Paula, Cal.	450
1928 Sept. 13	Lake Okeechobee, Fla.	2,000
1931 Aug.	Huang He River, China	3,700,000
1937 Jan. 22	Ohio, Miss. Valleys	250
1939	Northern China	200,000
1947	Honshu Island, Japan	1,900
1951 Aug.	Manchuria	1,800
1953 Jan. 31	Western Europe	2,000
1954 Aug. 17	Farahzad, Iran	2,000
1955 Oct. 7-12	India, Pakistan	1,700
1959 Nov. 1	Western Mexico	2,000
1959 Dec. 2	Frejus, France	412
1960 Oct. 10	Bangladesh	6,000
1960 Oct. 31	Bangladesh	4,000
1962 Feb. 17	German North Sea coast	343
1962 Sept. 27	Barcelona, Spain	445
1963 Oct. 9	Dam collapse, Vaiont, Italy	1,800
1966 Nov. 4-6	Florence, Venice, Italy	113
1967 Jan. 18-24	Eastern Brazil	894
1967 Mar. 19	Rio de Janeiro, Brazil	436
1968 Aug. 7-14	Gujarat State, India	1,000
1968 Oct. 7	Northeastern India	780
1969 Mar. 17	Mundau Valley, Alagoas, Brazil	218
1969 Aug. 25	Western Virginia	189
1969 Sept. 15	South Korea	250
1969 Oct. 1-8	Tunisia	500
1970 May 20	Central Romania	160
1970 July 22	Himalayas, India	500
1971 Feb. 26	Rio de Janeiro, Brazil	130
1972 Feb. 26	Buffalo Creek, W. Va.	118
1972 June 9	Rapid City, S.D.	236
1972 Aug. 7	Luzon Is., Philippines	454
1974 Mar. 29	Tubaro, Brazil	1,000
1974 Aug. 12	Monty-Long, Bangladesh	2,500
1975 Jan. 11	Southern Thailand	131
1976 June 5	Teton Dam collapse, Ida.	11
1976 July 31	Big Thompson Canyon, Col.	130
1976 Nov. 17	East Java, Indonesia	136
1977 July 19-20	Johnstown, Pa.	68
1978 June-Sept.	Northern India	1,200
1979 Jan.-Feb.	Brazil	204
1979 July	Lomblem Is., Indonesia	539
1979 Aug. 11	Morvi, India	5,000-15,000
1980 Feb. 13-22	So. Cal., Ariz.	26
1981 Apr.	Northern China	550
1981 July	Sichuan, Hubei Prov., China	1,300
1982 Jan. 23	Nr. Lima, Peru	600

Some Major Tornadoes Since 1925

Source: National Climatic Center, NOAA, U.S. Commerce Department

Date	Place	Deaths
1925 Mar. 18	Mo., Ill. Ind.	689
1926 Nov. 25	Belleville to Portland, Ark.	53
1927 Apr. 12	Rock Springs, Tex.	74
1927 May 9	Arkansas, Poplar Bluff, Mo.	92
1927 Sept. 29	St. Louis, Mo.	72
1929 Apr. 25	SE-Central Ga.	40
1930 May 6	Hill & Ellis Co., Tex.	41
1932 Mar. 21	Ala. (series of tornadoes)	268

Date		Place	Deaths	Date		Place	Deaths
1936	Apr. 5	Tupelo, Miss.	216	1959	Feb. 10	St. Louis, Mo.	21
1936	Apr. 6	Gainesville, Ga.	203	1960	May 5, 6	SE Oklahoma, Arkansas	30
1938	Sept. 29	Charleston, S.C.	32	1965	Apr. 11	Ind., Ill., Oh., Mich., Wis.	271
1942	Mar. 16	Central to NE Miss.	75	1966	Mar. 3	Jackson, Miss.	57
1942	Apr. 27	Rogers & Mayes Co., Okla.	52	1966	Mar. 3	Mississippi, Alabama	61
1944	June 23	Oh., Pa., W. Va., Md.	150	1967	Apr. 21	Illinois	33
1945	Apr. 12	Okla.-Ark.	102	1968	May 15	Arkansas	34
1947	Apr. 9	Tex., Okla. & Kan.	169	1969	Jan. 23	Mississippi	32
1948	Mar. 19	Bunker Hill & Gillespie, Ill.	33	1971	Feb. 21	Mississippi delta	110
1949	Jan. 3	La. & Ark.	58	1973	May 26-7	South, Midwest (series)	47
1952	Mar. 21	Ark., Mo., Tenn. (series)	208	1974	Apr. 3-4	Ala., Ga., Tenn., Ky., Oh.	350
1953	May 11	Waco, Tex.	114	1977	Apr. 1	Southeast Bangladesh	600
1953	June 8	Flint to Lakeport, Mich.	116	1977	Apr. 4	Ala., Miss., Ga.	22
1953	June 9	Worcester and vicinity, Mass.	90	1978	Apr. 16	Orissa, India	500
1953	Dec. 5	Vicksburg, Miss.	38	1979	Apr. 10	Tex., Okla.	60
1955	May 25	Udall, Kan.	80	1980	June 3	Grand Island, Neb. (series)	4
1957	May 20	Kan., Mo.	48	1982	Mar. 2-4	South, Midwest (series)	17
1958	June 4	Northwestern Wisconsin	30	1982	May 29	So. Ill.	15

Hurricanes, Typhoons, Blizzards, Other Storms

Names of hurricanes and typhoons in italics—H.—hurricane; T.—typhoon

Date	Location	Deaths	Date	Location	Deaths
1888 Mar. 11-14	Blizzard, Eastern U.S.	400	1965 Sept. 7-10	H.*Betsy*, Fla., Miss., La.	74
1900 Sept. 8	H., Galveston, Tex.	6,000	1965 Dec. 15	Windstorm, Bangladesh	10,000
1926 Sept. 16-22	H., Fla., Ala.	372	1966 June 4-10	H.*Alma*, Honduras, SE U.S.	51
1926 Oct. 20	H., Cuba	600	1966 Sept. 24-30	H.*Inez*, Carib., Fla., Mex.	293
1928 Sept. 12-17	H., W. Indies, Fla.	4,000	1967 July 9	T.*Billie*, Japan	347
1930 Sept. 3	H., San Domingo	2,000	1967 Sept. 5-23	H.*Beulah*, Carib., Mex., Tex.	54
1938 Sept. 21	H., New England	600	1967 Dec. 12-20	Blizzard, Southwest, U.S.	51
1942 Oct. 15-16	H., Bengal, India	11,000	1968 Nov. 18-28	T.*Nina*, Philippines	63
1944 Sept. 12-16	H., N.C. to New Eng.	389	1969 Aug. 17-18	H.*Camille*, Miss., La.	256
1953 Sept. 25-27	T., Vietnam, Japan	1,300	1970 July 30-		
1954 Aug. 30	H.*Carol*, Northeast U.S.	68	Aug. 5	H.*Celia*, Cuba, Fla., Tex.	31
1954 Oct. 12-13	H.*Hazel*, Eastern, U.S., Haiti	347	1970 Aug. 20-21	H.*Dorothy*, Martinique	42
1955 Aug. 12-13	H.*Connie*, Carolinas, Va., Md.	43	1970 Sept. 15	T.*Georgia*, Philippines	300
1955 Aug. 18-19	H.*Diane*, Eastern U.S.	400	1970 Oct. 14	T.*Sening*, Philippines	583
1955 Sept. 19	H.*Hilda*, Mexico	200	1970 Oct. 15	T.*Titang*, Philippines	526
1955 Sept. 22-28	H.*Janet*, Caribbean	500	1970 Nov. 13	Cyclone, Bangladesh	300,000 (est.)
1956 Feb. 1-29	Blizzard, Western Europe	1,000	1971 Aug. 1	T.*Rose*, Hong Kong	130
1957 June 27-30	H.*Audrey*, La., Tex.	430	1972 June 19-29	H.*Agnes*, Fla. to N.Y.	118
1958 Feb. 15-16	Blizzard, NE U.S.	171	1972 Dec. 3	T.*Theresa*, Philippines	169
1959 Sept. 17-19	T.*Sarah*, Far East	2,000	1973 June-Aug.	Monsoon rains in India	1,217
1959 Sept. 26-27	T.*Vera*, Honshu, Japan.	4,466	1974 June 11	Storm*Dinah*, Luzon Is., Philip.	71
1960 Sept. 4-12	H.*Donna*, Caribbean, E. U.S.	148	1974 July 11	T.*Gilda*, Japan, S. Korea.	108
1961 Oct. 31	H.*Hattie*, Br. Honduras	400	1974 Sept. 19-20	H.*Fifi*, Honduras.	2,000
1962 Feb. 17	Flooding, German Coast	343	1974 Dec. 25	Cyclone leveled Darwin, Aus.	50
1962 Sept. 27	Flooding, Barcelona, Spain	445	1975 Sept. 13-27	H.*Eloise*, Caribbean, NE U.S.	71
1963 May 28-29	Windstorm, Bangladesh	22,000	1976 May 20	T.*Olga*, floods, Philippines	215
1963 Oct. 4-8	H.*Flora*, Cuba, Haiti	6,000	1977 July 25, 31	T.*Thelma*, T.*Vera*, Taiwan	39
1964 Oct. 4-7	H.*Hilda*, La., Miss., Ga.	38	1978 Oct. 27	T.*Rita*, Philippines	c. 400
1964 June 30	T.*Winnie*, N. Philippines	107	1979 Aug. 30-		
1964 Sept. 5	T.*Ruby*, Hong Kong and China	735	Sept. 7	H.*David*, Caribbean, E U.S.	1,100
1964 Sept. 14	Flooding, central S. Korea	563	1980 Aug. 4-11	H.*Allen*, Caribbean, Texas	272
1964 Nov. 12	Flooding, S. Vietnam	7,000	1981 Nov. 25	T.*Irma*, Luzon Is., Philip.	176
1965 May 11-12	Windstorm, Bangladesh	17,000			
1965 June 1-2	Windstorm, Bangladesh	30,000			

Record Oil Spills

Name, place	Date	Cause	Tons
Ixtoc I oil well, southern Gulf of Mexico	June 3, 1979	Blowout	600,000
Atlantic Empress & Aegean Captain, off Trinidad & Tobago	July 19, 1979	Collision	300,000
Amoco Cadiz, near Portsall, France	March 16, 1978	Grounding	223,000
Torrey Canyon, off Land's End, England	March 18, 1967	Grounding	119,000
Sea Star, Gulf of Oman	Dec. 19, 1972	Collision	115,000
Urquiola, La Coruna, Spain	May 12, 1976	Grounding	100,000
Hawaiian Patriot, northern Pacific	Feb. 25, 1977	Fire	99,000
Othello, Tralhavet Bay, Sweden	March 20, 1970	Collision	60,000-100,000
Jacob Maersk, Porto do Leixoes, Portugal	Jan. 29, 1975	Grounding	84,000
Wafra, Cape Agulhas, South Africa	Feb. 27, 1971	Grounding	63,000
Epic Colacotroni, Caribbean	May 1975	Grounding	57,000

Other Notable Oil Spills

Source: Conservation Division, U.S. Geological Survey, U.S. Interior Department

Name, place	Date	Cause	Gallons
World Glory, off South Africa	June 13, 1968	Hull failure	13,524,000
Keo, off Massachusetts	Nov. 5, 1969	Hull failure	8,820,000
Storage tank, Sewaren, N.J.	Nov. 4, 1969	Tank rupture	8,400,000
Ekofisk oil field, North Sea	Apr. 22, 1977	Well blowout	8,200,000
Argo Merchant, Nantucket, Mass.	Dec. 15, 1976	Grounding	7,700,000
Pipeline, West Delta, La.	Oct. 15, 1967	Dragging anchor	6,720,000
Tanker off Japan	Nov. 30, 1971	Ship broke in half	6,258,000

has? You don't have to walk past all the shelves hoping you'll spot it by accident! There is an easier way. You can look up your report topic either in the card catalog or on microfiche.

The card catalog is a set of small drawers filled with index cards. There are cards for each book in the library. The cards are arranged alphabetically from A to Z. You can look up a book under either the title of the book or the author's last name. For instance, a book about earthquakes called *Danger from Below,* by Seymour Simon, has a title card under D for "Danger . . ." It has an author card under S for "Simon." In addition, book catalog cards are filed under the topic the book is about. This book also has a catalog card filed under E for "Earthquakes."

If you know the title or author of the book you want, you can look it up under either of these and find the book's Dewey Decimal Classification number. The number for *Danger from Below* is 551.2. But if you want to see what books the library has on your report topic, simply look under the name of the topic to find its number. Then you'll know where these books are located on the library shelves.

You may have trouble figuring out what the name of your topic is. If your report is on poodles, do you look up "poodles" or "dogs"? There may be no cards listed under "poodles." Then you can try the larger

SUBJECT CARD

EARTHQUAKES

551.2   Simon, Seymour
S   Danger from below; earthquakes: past,
       present, and future.   Four Winds
       [c1979]
       86p illus

       Investigates why earthquakes occur,
       where they can happen, and how they
       are predicted in addition to describ-
       ing great earthquakes throughout his-
       tory and ways to reduce damage from
       them in the future

       1 Earthquakes   I T

ISBN 0-590-07514-4

00048 *DC   002610   © THE BAKER & TAYLOR CO.   3033

TITLE CARD

Danger from below

551.2   Simon, Seymour
S   Danger from below; earthquakes: past,
       present, and future.   Four Winds
       [c1979]
       86p illus

       Investigates why earthquakes occur,
       where they can happen, and how they
       are predicted in addition to describ-
       ing great earthquakes throughout his-
       tory and ways to reduce damage from
       them in the future

       1 Earthquakes   I T

ISBN 0-590-07514-4

00048 *DC   002610   © THE BAKER & TAYLOR CO.   3033

AUTHOR CARD

551.2   Simon, Seymour
S   Danger from below; earthquakes: past,
       present, and future.   Four Winds
       [c1979]
       86p illus

       Investigates why earthquakes occur,
       where they can happen, and how they
       are predicted in addition to describ-
       ing great earthquakes throughout his-
       tory and ways to reduce damage from
       them in the future

       1 Earthquakes   I T

ISBN 0-590-07514-4

00048 *DC   002610   © THE BAKER & TAYLOR CO.   3033

heading "dogs." But sometimes books are listed under rather strange-sounding topics. If you can't find what you want, ask the librarian for help.

Instead of a card catalog, your library may have a microfiche system. In this system, all the catalog cards are photographed on sheets of microfilm that are easier to store. Looking up books on microfiche is exactly like looking them up in a card catalog, except that you use a projector to read the microfiche. If you've never used one of these projectors, ask the librarian to show you how.

Once you've found out where the books on your topic are located, go to the shelves and take a look at what's there. The title of a book gives you a clue about what's in it. As you read through the titles, you will see a number of books that don't sound very helpful. For example, if your topic is dinosaur fossils, a book entitled *Dinosaurs of North America* will be helpful, but the information will be limited to North America. You'll probably find several books that look useful. Take them over to a table and look inside. Then decide which books will help you with your topic.

At the beginning of a nonfiction book is a list of the chapter titles and the page numbers they begin on. This is called the table of contents. Read through the chapter titles. Do any of them seem to be just

Contents

This contents page, from *Cats: All About Them* by Alvin and Virginia Silverstein, is typical of contents pages that will be found at the beginning of nonfiction books.

what you're looking for? If so, this is a book to check out. For example, your report might be on Siamese cats. In a book entitled *Cats: All About Them,* Chapter 3, "Cat Breeds," will probably have information you want.

A book's index also tells you what information the book contains. An index is found on the last pages of many nonfiction books. It is an alphabetical listing of facts and ideas contained in the book, with the page numbers where you can find them. The index of this book tells you that Siamese cats are discussed on pages 68–71. Siamese kittens are mentioned on page 83.

Sometimes a table of contents doesn't tell you whether your topic is included in that book. At these times an index is especially helpful, because it lists everything the book talks about.

Checking a book's table of contents and index saves time. You don't have to read the whole book to find out whether it has the facts you need. This is a good way to choose the books you'll use for your research.

A portion of the index from *Cats: All About Them.*

□ FOUR □
Finding More Information

READING BOOKS is not the only way to learn about a topic. A museum may be just the place to gather information for your report. Many cities have several museums. If you don't know much about the museums where you live, check the Yellow Pages for the addresses and phone numbers. There is sure to be someone answering the phone who can give you information about when the museum is open and what kinds of things are in it. Some museums charge admission fees—be sure to ask about this and whether there is a discount for children your age.

A museum of natural history usually has exhibits about animals, plants, fish, and rocks. In fact, anything that has to do with the earth and its living creatures might be on exhibit. If you are doing a report on a topic like dinosaurs or giant redwoods or Eskimos, a natural history museum could be a good place to look for information.

Art museums often have other things besides paintings. Usually they exhibit sculpture and tapestries, or weavings. For a report on Egypt, take a look at the Egyptian pieces in the art museum. Seeing a real mummy case might give you a whole new idea for your report. Museum gift shops often have pictures of their exhibits on inexpensive postcards. You might find one that's just right for the cover of your report.

Local city or county museums often deal with the history of where you live. They have handcrafted items that were made nearby, exhibits about the environment of your area, and information about the people who first lived there. If you are doing a report on something that happened near your town, the local museum may have information about it.

There are lots of special museums scattered all over the country. Depending on where you live, you could be close to a museum of trains, ships, antique cars, stamps, ocean fish, comics, or almost anything else you can think of. These museums may be quite small, but the people who work in them are usually happy to help you find what you need.

Do you like to watch TV? Often you can find out facts for a report by watching a TV show. A special on penguins will give you lots of tips for a report on Antarctica. News specials during presidential election campaigns are a good source of information about how our system of government works. Televised international sports competitions, such as the Olympics, world championship skiing, swimming, or soccer, have interviews with young athletes about their training and home life. And of course, PBS shows like *Nova* are always packed with facts you can use in reports.

Think about your topic. Is there someone you can talk to who can give you firsthand information? In addition to reading about being a veterinarian or how to take care of a sick puppy, why not interview a vet in your town and find out what he or she has to say? If your topic is safety in the home, talking to a firefighter, police officer, and Red Cross first-aid instructor will probably give you enough information for a whole report.

Have you heard your grandfather talk about how he first came to the United States as a boy? Maybe the lady next door likes to tell you what your town was like long before you were born. When you listen to these people, you are hearing oral history. This is history that is told, not written in books. The facts and details these people remember often are not in any books. And you can ask whatever questions you like. A book doesn't answer you the way a real live person does. Listening to oral history makes the past come alive. You will feel as though you had been there yourself.

Everyone you talk to knows a lot about something. But the person who has special information for your report could be you! If your teacher assigns national parks as a topic, why not write about one you've been to? You'll need to get some of the facts from reference books. But these books can't tell you what it feels like to hike down the Bright Angel Trail in the Grand Canyon, get sprayed by a geyser at Yellowstone, or touch Spanish moss hanging from the trees in the Everglades. Including your own memories or experiences in your report can make it extra exciting.

Pretend you're a detective! As you search for information on your topic, imagine other places you might look. People are usually glad to help you. Don't be afraid to explore ideas for research. You might uncover a gold mine!

□ FIVE □
What Do You Want to Know?

Sometimes It Seems That there are *too* many places to look for information. It's hard to figure out where to start. Before you run off to the library or ask someone for an interview, think about your topic. The reason you chose this topic is that you would like to know more about it. What exactly do you want to know?

If the topic is dinosaurs and you've read that some scientists now think they may have been warm-blooded, you might do your report on warm-blooded dinosaurs. What questions could you ask to get the information you want? First, did warm-blooded dinosaurs really exist? What did they look like? What makes scientists think they were warm-blooded? What does "warm-blooded" mean, anyway? The answers to these questions will be the information you need to write your report.

How will you keep track of all this information? You need to take notes. There are lots of different ways of taking notes. Some people use index cards, some use notebook paper, some scribble on little scraps of paper and then lose them in the laundry! But one easy way to keep track of your notes is to make a large chart.

Use a big piece of paper. You can cut open a large grocery bag so it lies flat, or use a length of shelf paper. Brown wrapping paper that was used to wrap a package also works well. In fact, any kind of paper that's big enough is fine. On brown paper it's best to write with a felt-tip pen so you'll be able to read your notes easily.

Divide the paper into columns—you'll need one column for each question you want to answer, plus a column to list the books you use. A ruler or yardstick will help you keep the lines neat and clear. Make the boxes large enough for two or three sentences. Write one of your questions at the top of each empty column.

In the first column, write down the name of each book you are using and the name of its author. Also write down the date the book was published. This information is found on the copyright page of the book, on the back of the title page. For example, if you look at the back of the title page of this book, you will see that it was published in 1983. (You can use the copyright date as the date of publication. In most cases, they are the same date.) If you are interviewing someone, write down his or her name and phone number and the date of the interview in the first column.

Now you are ready to start taking notes. In your first research book, find the paragraphs or sections that talk about your topic. As you read, keep your questions in mind. Look for the information that answers your question. Write it down in the correct box.

Do the same for each book you read or person you talk to. When your chart is filled, you will be able to see at a glance what information you have about each of your questions.

WARM-BLOODED DINOSAURS

	Did they exist?	What does warm-blooded mean?	What makes scientists think they were warm-blooded?	What did the warm-blooded dinosaurs look like?
The New Book of Knowledge 1978				
Merit Students Encyclopedia 1980				
Dictionary of Dinosaurs, Joseph Rosenbloom 1980				
The Warm-Blooded Dinosaurs, Julian May 1978				
Conclusions				

□ SIX □

Taking Notes

NOTES ARE REMINDERS of what you've read or heard. They keep you from getting mixed up about who said what. You won't forget an important fact if it's in your notes.

You can write your notes either as whole sentences or as short phrases. Just make sure that your notes are not as long as the book you are reading! You should be able to sum up the main idea of a paragraph in one or two sentences. Suppose you read this paragraph:

However, some scientists do not believe that dinosaurs were cold-blooded reptiles. They think dinosaurs may have been warm-blooded, or partially warm-blooded. But nobody knows for sure.

Dictionary of Dinosaurs,
Joseph Rosenbloom, page 7

Your notes might look like those on the next page:

WARM-BLOODED DINOSAURS

	Did they exist?	What does warm-blooded mean?	What makes scientists think they were warm-blooded?	What did the warm-blooded dinosaurs look like?
The New Book of Knowledge 1978				
Merit Students Encyclopedia 1980				
Dictionary of Dinosaurs, Joseph Rosenbloom 1980	Some scientists think so, but no one really knows.			
The Warm-Blooded Dinosaurs, Julian May 1978				
Conclusions				

You can even use abbreviations of long words to save space. You might write "dino" for "dinosaur." And "w-b" and "c-b" could stand for "warm-blooded" and "cold-blooded." It's best to abbreviate only the words that are used often in your notes. That way you won't forget what each abbreviation stands for.

Remember that you are reading to find out answers to the questions at the top of your chart. So you don't have to sum up everything the book's author says. Only take notes on the information that helps answer your questions.

Your notes should be written in your own words, not copied from the book. After you've read a paragraph or short section of information on your topic, mark your place with a slip of paper and close the book. Now write down the main idea in your own words.

Why should you close the book to take notes? There are two reasons. First, this is a way of making sure you understand what you have read. It's pretty hard to write a report if you don't really understand the information you've collected. But you know you've got the idea when you can explain it your own way.

The other reason is that your report should be your own work. Copying from a book or from several books is not the same as writing a report. It may seem easier to write down the exact words of a book on your note chart. But you will use the words in your notes when you sit down to write your report. And you won't remember then that these are another author's words, not your own. When your notes are in your own words, you can use these sentences in your report.

Of course, changing the words doesn't mean that you change the facts. If you read that a dinosaur called Allosaurus weighed between three and four tons, you can't say it weighed one ton. That would be making up a new "fact," and it wouldn't be true.

Facts belong to everybody. The weight of a dinosaur is a fact that anyone can read about and use. Putting the facts you learn in your report is not stealing. But you cannot write them in exactly the same way another author has. You can't pretend that someone else's sentences are your own. (If you do use sentences from a book, you must put quotation marks around them and tell your reader where you read them.)

As you take notes, remember that library books do not belong to you. When you close the book to write down a main idea in your notes, use a slip of paper to mark your place. Don't bend down the corner of the page. And never write anything in a library book. There's nothing more annoying than trying to read a book that someone else has marked up!

You also need to take notes when you talk to someone to get information for your report. Use the same kind of chart, and write down the answers to your questions as you listen.

Most people are happy to share their knowledge. But since you'll be taking up their time, try to get organized beforehand. When you make an appointment to talk to someone, be on time. Bring your own pencil and chart for notes. And be prepared with your questions. Also, don't forget to say thank you at the end of the interview. It never hurts to be polite. You might need to go back for a second interview!

SEVEN

Getting Ready to Write

ONCE YOU HAVE WRITTEN all your notes on your chart, you are ready to organize your information. What conclusions can you come to?

Look at all the notes in the first column, which are the answers to your first question. Do they all say more or less the same thing? If so, write a sentence in the bottom box of that column that tells the main idea. Do the same for each column in your chart.

This can be tricky. You may have found different answers to your questions in the research books you read. When authors don't agree, you can't just count up the yes's and no's to see which answer has the most votes!

There are many reasons why authors disagree

WARM-BLOODED DINOSAURS

	Did they exist?	What does warm-blooded mean?	What makes scientists think they were warm-blooded?	What did the warm-blooded dinosaurs look like?
The New Book of Knowledge 1978	No		Dinosaurs were reptiles, so therefore they were cold-blooded. They lived a slow-moving life.	
Merit Students Encyclopedia 1980	Some say yes, but no one is sure.		They were active and fast, so they must have had a lot of body heat. But maybe the sun warmed them enough for short periods of moving fast.	
Dictionary of Dinosaurs, Joseph Rosenbloom 1980	Some scientists think so, but no one really knows. Scientists are starting to think dinosaurs were very active, not like reptiles of today.		Running fast takes more energy than cold-blooded animals have. C-b animals can't do anything if the weather is too hot or too cold.	Fastest one, Ornithomimus, looked like an ostrich.

			Many had large leg muscles for running fast. Some were very large. Their skeletons look a lot like bird skeletons.
		Fossils show that they fought a lot, which takes energy. Some big ones lived in cold climates. Their bones (fossils) have many blood-vessel holes, like the bones of warm-blooded animals.	
	Cold-blooded means body is same temperature as air or water it is in. Reptiles are c-b. Large ones can't survive in cold climates. W-b. means blood stays the same temp., no matter what air or water temp. is. Body has built-in way of keeping temp. even.		
The Warm-Blooded Dinosaurs, Julian May 1978	In 1972 Robert T. Bakker from Harvard decided dinosaurs must have been w-b. Some other scientists agreed with him.		
Conclusions			

about a topic. New information may have been discovered about your topic. A book that was published
before this information was discovered won't men-
tion it. Even a recent book won't have this information if its author didn't hear about it. For example,
scientists used to think that Brontosaurus had a
short, blunt snout. But a few years ago a real Brontosaurus head was discovered. It was longer and
thinner. Books that were published before this dis-
covery have pictures of Brontosaurus with the wrong
kind of head.

Sometimes scientists come up with a new idea or
theory about how something happened. Until they
prove that the theory is true, some people will believe
it and some won't. This means that books on this
topic may disagree.

When you find disagreement between the answers to one of your questions, you may need two
sentences for the bottom box of that column. For the
chart on page 56, the sentences in the first bottom box
could be:

Scientists used to think all dinosaurs were cold-blooded.
Now some scientists think some dinosaurs were warm-
blooded.

There are other times when you might find different answers to one of your questions. For instance,

one book on dog care says puppies that are less than four months old have to be paper trained. But when you interview a woman who runs dog training classes, she says that puppies should be trained to go to the bathroom outdoors as soon as they are old enough to leave their mothers.

The author of the dog care book and the woman who teaches the classes both know a lot about dogs. Maybe both of them are right. They disagree on the best way to train a puppy, but they agree that puppies can be trained in some way. Your sentences in the box at the bottom of this column might be:

Puppies can be trained to go to the bathroom outdoors. They can also be paper trained.

There won't be any disagreement in your notes on some topics. But if there is, try to figure out what the disagreement means. Perhaps both books are partly right. Or maybe you can think of a reason why one book is wrong. What you say about this is part of what makes the report your own, not just a copy of the books you've read.

Now that the boxes at the bottom of your chart are filled in, you are ready to decide how your report will be organized. In some ways writing a report is like telling a story. Your report will have a beginning, a middle, and an end.

WARM-BLOODED DINOSAURS

	Did they exist?	What does warm-blooded mean?	What makes scientists think they were warm-blooded?	What did the warm-blooded dinosaurs look like?
The New Book of Knowledge 1978				
Merit Students Encyclopedia 1980				
Dictionary of Dinosaurs, Joseph Rosenbloom 1980				
The Warm-Blooded Dinosaurs, Julian May 1978				
Conclusions	Scientists used to think all dinosaurs were cold-blooded. Now some scientists think some dinosaurs were warm-blooded.	Warm-blooded means that the body is always the same temperature.	If dinosaurs were cold-blooded, they wouldn't have had enough energy to live the way they did.	They were built for speed, and some were very large.

For some topics, deciding what comes first is easy. If your report tells how to make chocolate chip cookies, the first information the reader needs is the list of ingredients. Next you explain, in the right order, the steps for mixing up the ingredients. Then you tell how to put the dough on the cookie sheet and how long and at what temperature to bake the cookies. Last you could tell how good they taste when they're done. Whenever you are telling how to do something—housetrain a puppy, build a model, or learn to be a lifeguard—you will quickly see that there is a natural order to follow.

The order in which you write about other kinds of topics may be harder to figure out. A report on warm-blooded dinosaurs can be organized in a couple of different ways. Probably the first part of the report should answer the question *Did warm-blooded dinosaurs exist?* Then you could explain what "warm-blooded" means. Next you might tell why scientists are beginning to think that dinosaurs were warm-blooded instead of cold-blooded. And finally you could give some information about what these dinosaurs looked like. This is the same order as the questions at the top of the notes chart.

But there is another way to organize this report. It would begin in the same way, with the answers to the first two questions from the chart. But you might decide to tell what the dinosaurs looked like next, and end your report with an explanation of why some scientists now think the dinosaurs were warm-blooded.

Either way you decided to organize this report on warm-blooded dinosaurs would make sense to the reader. The important point to keep in mind is that you are the person who has the information. You are trying to pass it on to your reader. Think of what things the reader needs to know first. Pretend you are explaining your topic to a friend who doesn't know anything about it. What would you have to say first so your friend could understand the rest of your explanation?

The sentences in the bottom boxes of each column of your chart are the main ideas for each paragraph or section of your report. Once you have figured out what order you think your information should be written in, list these main ideas in that order on a piece of paper. Be sure to leave some space between each one. Then you can put whatever details you have under the main ideas. This list is an outline. It will be a kind of map for you to follow when you write your report.

Most reports need an ending paragraph. This can be a summary of what you've said in your report. Another way to end is to tell why your topic is an interesting one. Whatever way you decide to end your report, be sure to add a sentence to the end of your outline so you will remember what you planned to say.

You may wonder whether all this work is necessary. Wouldn't it be easier to just start writing and hope for the best? The answer is no. When you think about your topic and the questions you plan to answer in your report, you get a clear idea in your mind of what you want to say. This makes it easier to write your report. And if you get confused, you can always look at your chart or list to remind yourself of what you wanted to say next.

OUTLINE

Were Dinosaurs Warm-blooded?

I. Scientists used to think all dinosaurs were cold-blooded. Now some scientists think some dinosaurs were warm-blooded.

    A. In 1972 Robert T. Bakker from Harvard decided that dinosaurs must have been warm-blooded.

    B. Other scientists agreed with him.

    C. But it is still not really proved.

    D. Maybe it can't ever be proved.

II. Warm-blooded means that the body is always the same temperature.

    A. The body has a built-in way of keeping its temperature even, no matter what the air or water is like.

    B. This is very different from cold-blooded, which means the body becomes the same temperature as the air or water around it.

    C. Cold-blooded animals slow down and hibernate when the weather is cold.

III. Many dinosaurs were built for speed, and some were very large.

    A. They had very large leg muscles, which means they must have been able to run fast.

    B. Their skeletons look like bird skeletons, and birds are warm-blooded.

C.   Some were shaped like birds.

D.   The fastest one, Ornithomimus, looked like an ostrich.

IV.   If dinosaurs were cold-blooded, they wouldn't have had enough energy to live the way they did.

A.   Scientists used to think dinosaurs were very slow-moving.

B.   Now some people disagree. They think the dinosaurs ran fast to chase others for food or to get away.

C.   Fossils show that they fought each other a lot.

D.   Running and fighting takes lots of energy, and cold-blooded animals wouldn't be able to do these things.

E.   Some lived in cold climates. This must have made them slow if they were cold-blooded. But they were fast.

F.   Some people think the sun made them warm enough to move fast, but they could only move fast for short periods of time.

G.   Their bones have lots of holes for blood vessels. This is like the bones of warm-blooded animals, not cold-blooded.

V.   *Summary Sentence:*   Bakker's idea may change people's minds about prehistoric times.

□ EIGHT □

Writing Your Report

YOU ARE NOW READY to write your report. When your teacher first talked to the class about report writing, he or she may have given you some rules about how to write reports. If so, you will want to follow these rules. Certainly your teacher told you that reports must be written neatly. If they aren't, no one can read them! It is important to write carefully to make sure that what you have to say can be read by anyone.

Make sure also that you know how this report is supposed to look. Are you going to make a cover? Should you draw a map or pictures to put in it? How long should the report be? Look at the box below to remind yourself of other things your teacher may have said.

The sentences that are in the bottom boxes of your chart can be the first sentences, or topic sen-

How many pages, or how many paragraphs?
Pencil or pen?
Write on every line, or skip every other line?
Write on one side of the paper, or both sides?
Where should you put the page numbers
on each page?
Where should you write your
name on each page?

tences, of paragraphs in your report. The topic sentence gives a general idea of what that paragraph will be about. The rest of each paragraph will give details or explanations about this idea or fact.

As you write each paragraph, try to say things as clearly as you can. You want the reader to understand what you've learned about your topic. Again, pretend you are explaining it to a friend. Say a sentence out loud and then write down the words you've just said.

When you talk to someone, you use different kinds of sentences. It's a good idea to do that when you write, too. Sentences that all start the same way are boring. Make your report more interesting to read. How about beginning or ending a paragraph with a question?

When you finish each paragraph, stop to look it over. Did you say what you meant to say? Did you include everything you wanted to include? Is the paragraph clear and understandable? If the answer to any of these questions is no, now is the time to change things. There is nothing wrong with crossing out what you've written and redoing it to make it better. People who write books and magazine articles do this all the time.

Look back at your outline. This is a way of checking to make sure you've put in all the details you planned to. If you have, you can check off that section and move on to the next paragraph.

Here is the way one person used the notes and outline about warm-blooded dinosaurs to write a report. As you read it, maybe you'll think of ways it could have been better. Keep these thoughts in mind when you write your own report.

Each report you do will be easier to write than the one before. It will also be better. You've probably heard that "practice makes perfect," and it's true! As you practice doing research, organizing your ideas, and writing reports, you'll get better and better at it. Like playing baseball or playing the violin, writing is a skill that you can learn only by doing.

Jennifer Green
November 3, 1983

Were Dinosaurs Warm-blooded?

Scientists used to think all dinosaurs were cold-blooded. Now some scientists think some dinosaurs were warm-blooded. In 1972 a scientist from Harvard, Robert T. Bakker, said something that surprised people. He said that dinosaurs must have been warm-blooded. When he explained why he thought this, many scientists agreed with him.

Other scientists didn't think he had proved that dinosaurs were warm-blooded. It's hard to know what dinosaurs were like because they lived so long ago. But these scientists still believe that they were cold-blooded.

Warm-blooded means that the body is always the same temperature. Warm-blooded animals have a built-in way of keeping their body temperature even. It doesn't matter what temperature the air or water is. This is different from cold-blooded animals. Their bodies become the same temperature as the air or water around them. Cold-blooded animals slow down and hibernate when the weather is cold. But warm-blooded animals keep moving around in the cold weather.

What did warm-blooded dinosaurs look like? Some were very large. Many of them were built for speed. They had very large leg muscles. This means they must have been able to run fast. The fastest one, Ornithomimus, looked like an ostrich. Some of the others were also shaped like birds. Their skeletons look like bird skeletons. Birds are warm-blooded.

Scientists have many reasons for believing that dinosaurs were warm-blooded. Here are some of them. First, if dinosaurs were cold-blooded, they wouldn't have had

Jennifer Green

enough energy to live the way they did. Scientists used to think dinosaurs were very slow moving because they were so big. But now some scientists don't think that. They think the dinosaurs ran fast to chase others for food or to get away. These scientists say fossils show that dinosaurs fought each other a lot. Dinosaur bones have teeth marks from other dinosaurs to prove this.

It takes lots of energy to run and fight. If dinosaurs were cold-blooded they wouldn't have been able to do these things. Cold-blooded animals need heat from the sun to give them energy. But some fast-moving dinosaurs lived in cold climates. If they were cold-blooded, they would have been slow.

The scientists who think all dinosaurs were cold-blooded say that there was enough sun to let dinosaurs run and fight for short periods of time. But the people who think some dinosaurs were warm-blooded say that the fast ones ran and fought all the time.

There is another reason some scientists think dinosaurs were warm-blooded. Dinosaurs bones have lots of holes in them for blood vessels. Warm-blooded animals' bones have lots of holes in them for blood vessels, but cold-blooded animals' bones' don't have very many.

Dinosaurs have been extinct for a very long time. Scientists have studied dinosaurs' bones for many years. But Robert Bakker had his idea about dinosaurs being warm-blooded only a few years ago. If he is right, many people will have to change what they think about prehistoric times.

□ NINE □
Checking Your Report

FINALLY YOU HAVE FINISHED writing your report. But there is one more important step before you hand it in. Checking over your report doesn't take long. And this is how you make sure that all the work you did was worth it. You've done a great job so far. Take time now to polish up your report. You want it to look its best!

Does your report say just what you wanted to say? Read it out loud, either to yourself or to someone else. You'll notice right away if something sounds strange. Maybe some of your sentences are not complete. Put in the missing words. Or you may have a sentence that seems to run on forever. Split it into two or more shorter ones. As you read, the person listening can tell you if he or she has trouble understanding any parts of your report. This will let you know that those parts need to be fixed.

Try trading reports with a friend for a final check. When you read what you wrote yourself, it's often hard to catch mistakes. After all, you know what you meant to say when you wrote it. Another person may be able to see misspelled words that you have missed or places where you forgot to put in capital letters or punctuation marks. And having a friend read your report will let you know that at least one other person can read your handwriting!

Don't forget that neatness counts. If there are a lot of mistakes that you need to correct, it might be a good idea to copy that whole page over. When your report is neatly written, your teacher will be able to think about what it says instead of trying to figure out what each word is supposed to be. Look at the box below for a reminder of things to check in your report.

EXTRAS

Does your report need a cover? Would a picture help people understand what your report is about? Some reports don't need anything but words. But sometimes a good report can be even better with something extra.

Indent the first line of every paragraph.

Begin each sentence with a capital letter.

End each sentence with a period, question mark, or exclamation mark.

Check your spelling.

Check for missing words.

Number your pages.

Can you read your handwriting?

Would a map be helpful? Your report might be about where dinosaur bones were found, where your grandparents were born, where you went on vacation, or where Eskimos live. A map might tell more about these topics than you can say in words. Trace or copy your map from an atlas, or see if you can find one to cut out of a magazine. Don't forget to label any maps you draw.

If you found inexpensive pictures for your report at a museum gift shop or stationery store, be sure to put them in. Maybe you found a magazine picture showing something about your topic. And you can always draw your own pictures. Check out a library book with good illustrations. Use them as your models or trace pictures from the book. If your pictures are on small pieces of paper, paste them to whole sheets of paper so they won't fall out of your report.

A cover can be made out of almost any kind of paper. Construction paper, typing paper, and even notebook paper make fine report covers. A report on how food gets from farm to supermarket would look great with a cover made from a brown-paper shopping bag. And the cover for a report on what it's like to be a newspaper reporter could be made from the front page of your local newspaper. Paste it on notebook paper to keep it from tearing. For a report on a holiday, make a cover out of gift-wrapping paper with an appropriate holiday theme.

If your report is longer than one page, you will need some way to hold it together so the pages don't get lost. Anything that goes with the look of the rest of your report is fine, unless your teacher has told you how it should be done. You can staple the pages and cover together along the left edge, or use a paper clip in the upper left corner. Or try tying the pages together with yarn through punched holes so that it looks like an old-fashioned scrapbook.

At last your report is ready to be handed in. It's filled with the interesting information you've gathered, as well as your own ideas. The pages are neatly written and the spelling is correct. Everything has been checked. Be sure your name is on the cover and on every page—this is a report you can be proud of!

□ TEN □
Recommendations for Your Study Space

Writing a Report is much easier if you have a good place to work. It doesn't have to be a whole room of your own. Maybe you share a room and a desk, or maybe you do your homework on the kitchen table. Wherever your study space is, you need:
- a smooth, flat surface to write on
- good light for reading and writing
- a chair that's the right height for your desk
- study tools, like scratch paper, good paper, pencils, pens, eraser, and ruler

With this equipment, you have a good start on doing your best work.

YOUR REFERENCE SHELF

As you go on in school and do more writing, you'll want to have some reference books of your own. Maybe you already have a dictionary. Keep it in your study space so that it will be handy when you want to use it. If you don't have one, why not ask for one for your birthday or Christmas? There are other kinds of reference books that are nice to own. You don't need to get them all at once, but here are some you might want in the future.

Dictionary

Use a dictionary to make sure you spell words correctly in your report. You can also look up the exact meaning of a word you want to use. What kind of dictionary do you need? Dictionaries that are written especially for elementary school students are easy to read and to use. The ones for older students and adults are harder to read, but they have more words in them. A good way to pick out the kind of dictionary you want is to look at several different ones in a library or bookstore. Try looking up the same word in each one. Then you can see which definition is the most helpful. Here are some dictionaries written for students:

> *Children's Dictionary,* published by American Heritage, Houghton Mifflin Company, Boston.
>
> *Macmillan Dictionary for Children,* published by Macmillan Publishing Company, Inc., New York.
>
> *Scott, Foresman Beginning Dictionary,* Doubleday Edition, published by Doubleday and Company, Inc., Garden City, New York.
>
> *Webster's New World Dictionary for Young Readers,* published by Simon & Schuster, Inc.
>
> *Webster's New Collegiate Dictionary,* published by G. & C. Merriam Company, Springfield, Massachusetts (this desk-size dictionary is used by high school and college students).

Unabridged dictionaries are expensive, but can be a good investment. Before purchasing, it's a good idea to visit a library or bookstore that has a good, up-to-date reference section. Look at the contents page to see what each dictionary contains other than word definitions. For instance, *The Random House Dictionary of the English Language,* Unabridged Edition (published by Random House, Inc., New York) has a 64-page color atlas, concise dictionaries of French, Spanish, Italian, and German, and several other extra features. *Webster's Third New International Dictionary* (published by G. & C. Merriam Company, Springfield, Massachusetts) has several useful lists, such as constellations and stars, and color plates inserted throughout illustrating butterflies, flags, birds, etc. Since both have good reputations as dictionaries, perhaps your choice will be based on which one has extra features that you think will be most useful to you.

Thesaurus

A thesaurus is a dictionary of synonyms. Synonyms are words that have the same or similar meanings. It's good to have one so you won't keep using the same words over and over again. Some thesauruses are complicated to use, even for adults! Here are two that are written for students:

> *The Clear and Simple Thesaurus Dictionary* by Harriet Wittels and Joan Greisman, published by Grosset & Dunlap, Inc., New York.
>
> *Junior Thesaurus: In Other Words II* by Andrew Schiller and William A. Jenkins, published by Lothrop, Lee & Shepard Books, New York.

Atlas

It's nice to have an atlas at home so you don't have to go to the library every time you want to look at a map. There are lots of different kinds of atlases. Some of them are very expensive. Two that have maps of the whole world and are not very expensive are:

> *The Hammond Citation World Atlas,* published in paperback by Hammond, Inc., New York

The World Atlas, published in paperback by the Random House Library of Knowledge, New York.

Almanac

These books are filled with all sorts of information. Some are rewritten every year so they have all the up-to-date facts. These are usually hard to read because the type is so small. Other almanacs, written for students, do not come out every year. Here are some of each to look at:

The Hammond Almanac (yearly editions)

Information Please Almanac (yearly editions)

The World Almanac and Book of Facts (yearly editions published by Newspaper Enterprise Association, Inc., New York.)

Macmillan Illustrated Almanac for Kids, published by Macmillan Publishing Company, Inc., New York.

Other Useful Books

There are many other books that can help you with your studies. A book written for elementary and junior high school students that contains lots of helpful hints is:

How to Sharpen Your Study Skills by Sigmund Kalina, published by Lothrop, Lee & Shepard Books, New York.

And why not ask your teacher for suggestions? He or she may know about other books that are especially helpful.

Good luck, and have fun writing great school reports!

Index

About the Authors

ELIZABETH JAMES and CAROL BARKIN are experienced writers who had to learn the hard way that organization and planning are the two main ingredients in good writing. *How to Write a Great School Report* is the book they wish had been available to help them when they first began writing in elementary school.

ELIZABETH JAMES received her B.A. in mathematics from Colorado College, where she minored in experimental psychology. She and her husband live in Beverly Hills, California.

CAROL BARKIN received her B.A. from Radcliffe College, where she majored in English. Formerly a children's book editor, Ms. Barkin is now a full-time writer. She and her husband live in Hastings-on-Hudson, New York, with their young son.

JAMES and BARKIN have written many books together. Among them is *How to Write a Term Paper* for high school students, about which the *Bulletin of the Center for Children's Books* at the University of Chicago has said: "In an excellent how-to book, James and Barkin strike a nice balance between a serious approach and a light style. . . . The material is logically organized and clearly explained—not just what to do but why. . . . Recommended."